HOWARD GOODALL

CHRISTMAS CANTATA

for soprano solo, SATB choir, organ
and chamber orchestra

(2019)

VOCAL SCORE

© 2021 by Faber Music Ltd
First published in 2021 by Faber Music Ltd
Bloomsbury House, 74–77 Great Russell Street, London WC1B 3DA
Cover design by Adam Hay Studio
Music processed by Donald Thomson and the composer
Printed in England by Caligraving Ltd
All rights reserved

ISBN10: 0-571-54094-5
EAN13: 978-0-571-54094-5

Permission to perform this work in public must be obtained from the Society
duly controlling performing rights unless there is a current licence for public performance
from the Society in force in relation to the premises at which the performance is to take place.
Such permission must be obtained in the UK from
www.prsformusic.com

Christmas Cantata was first performed by the choirs of St Luke's United Methodist Church,
Houston, Texas (Director of Music and Fine Arts, Sid Davis), on 15 December 2019,
conducted by Howard Goodall CBE, with soloist Grace Roman.

The première performances were supported by St Luke's Friends of Music.

Romance of the Angels originally commissioned by the BBC Singers
To See Another Sun originally commissioned by St Mary's, Barnes
Romance of the Epiphany and *Lullaby of Winter* originally commissioned by Christ Church Cathedral Choir, Oxford
I Am Christmas Day originally commissioned by Mercy Ships UK

Duration: *c.*40 mins

Instrumentation

Flute

Oboe

Clarinet in B♭

Bassoon

2 Horns in F

2 Trumpets in B♭

Percussion (2 Players)
sleigh bells; suspended cymbal; glockenspiel; maracas; finger cymbal;
snare drum; triangle; bass drum; mark/bell tree; timpani

Harp

Piano (doubling Celesta)

Organ*

Strings

*or digital keyboard if a tuned pipe organ is unavailable.

Parts available on hire from the publishers (hire@fabermusic.com)

To buy Faber Music publications or to find out about the full range of titles available
please contact your local music retailer or Faber Music sales enquiries:

Faber Music Limited, Burnt Mill, Elizabeth Way, Harlow, CM20 2HX England
Tel: +44 (0)1279 82 89 82
fabermusic.com

Composer's note

Christmas means many things to different people around the world. The nativity story itself was brought to the centre of the celebration by Franciscan priests in medieval Italy, with the addition of sung, festive carols and makeshift mangers. This was a (highly successful) effort to encourage farming communities, especially isolated hill- and mountain-dwelling shepherds and goatherds, to join church services. Hence the newly boosted narrative role for shepherds and their flocks in a story set in an arid desert landscape.

For me, the nativity story – however literally one addresses its mix of anecdotal, historical, mythical and blurred-by-time details – carries a very powerful, universal message. It tells of a poor mother and her child, in difficult, fragile circumstances, seeking refuge in an unfamiliar place. They are not reduced to a footnote of the tale but made the very epicentre and purpose of it. The smallest, least important people, usually at the edge of the frame, stand centre-stage. Power is transferred from a mighty empire to a child.

We have been reminded in recent years of the significance and potential of immensely courageous children, from Malala Yousafzai to Greta Thunberg. So the subtext of the nativity is clear to us, whether or not we believe the child in question was in some sense a manifestation, offspring, or representative of God.

This cantata's underlying theme, therefore, is that the joy of hope is expressed in this famous birth as representative of all births, that children are the beacons of our future and that caring for the vulnerable, the needy and the displaced has never been more urgent and germane.

"When I am there to help relieve an unknown person's grief
To share the load, whatever their belief
I am Christmas Day"

Howard Goodall CBE, July 2021

VOCAL SCORE

CHRISTMAS CANTATA

1. Romance of the Angels

Romance que cantó la novena orden, que son los seraphines

Fray Iñigo de Mendoza (late 15th century)
Trans. Howard Goodall

Howard Goodall

Go - zo mu - es - tren en la tie - rra y en el lim - bo a - leg-

© 2012 by Faber Music Ltd.
This edition © 2021 by Faber Music Ltd.

1. Romance of the Angels

1. Romance of the Angels

1. Romance of the Angels

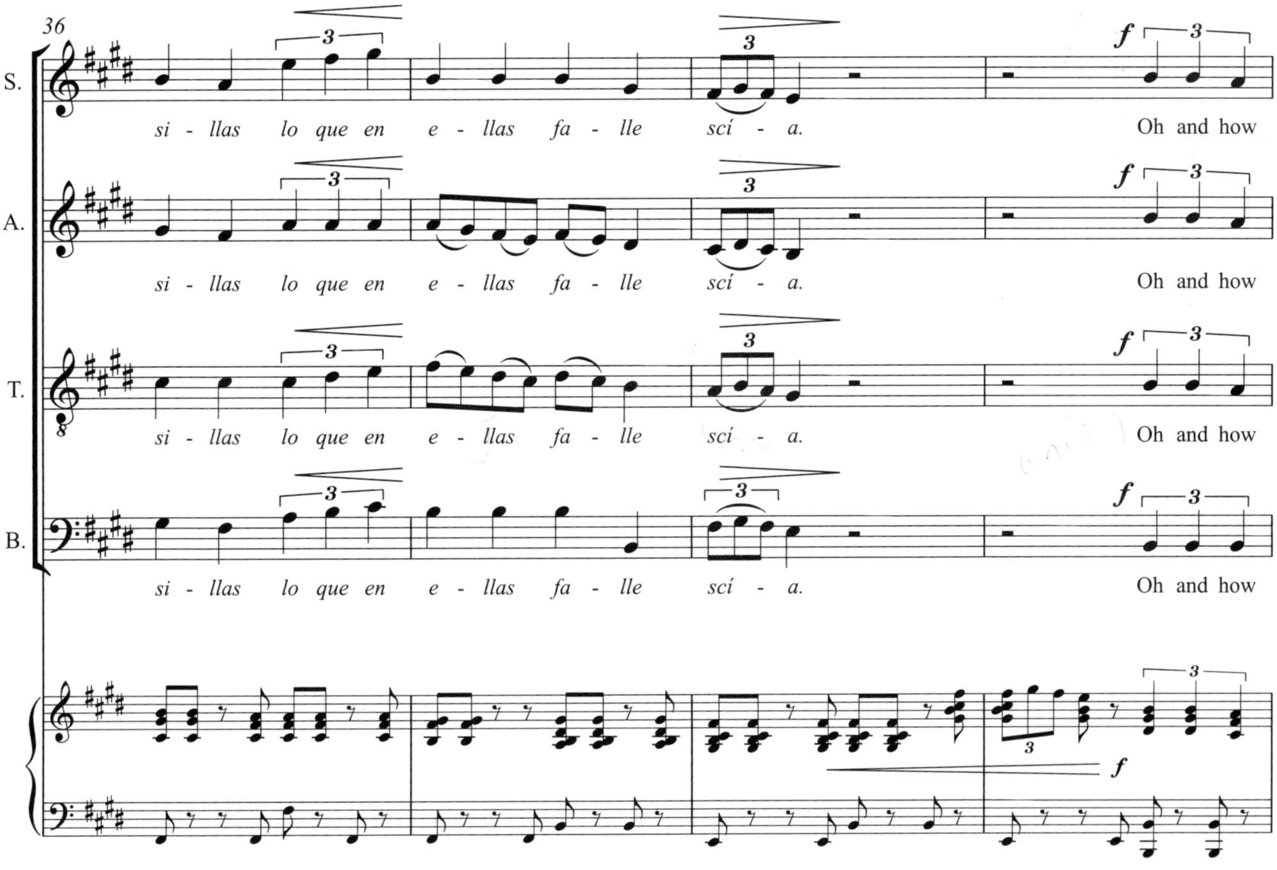
36
S.
si - llas lo que en e - llas fa - lle scí - a. Oh and how
A.
si - llas lo que en e - llas fa - lle scí - a. Oh and how
T.
si - llas lo que en e - llas fa - lle scí - a. Oh and how
B.
si - llas lo que en e - llas fa - lle scí - a. Oh and how

40
S.
great the pow'r of love since by such gen - tle per - se - ve - rance love not
A.
great the pow'r of love___ since by such gen - tle per - se - ve - rance love not
T.
great the pow'r of love since by such gen - tle per - se - ve - rance love not
B.
great the pow'r of love since by such gen - tle per - se - ve - rance love not

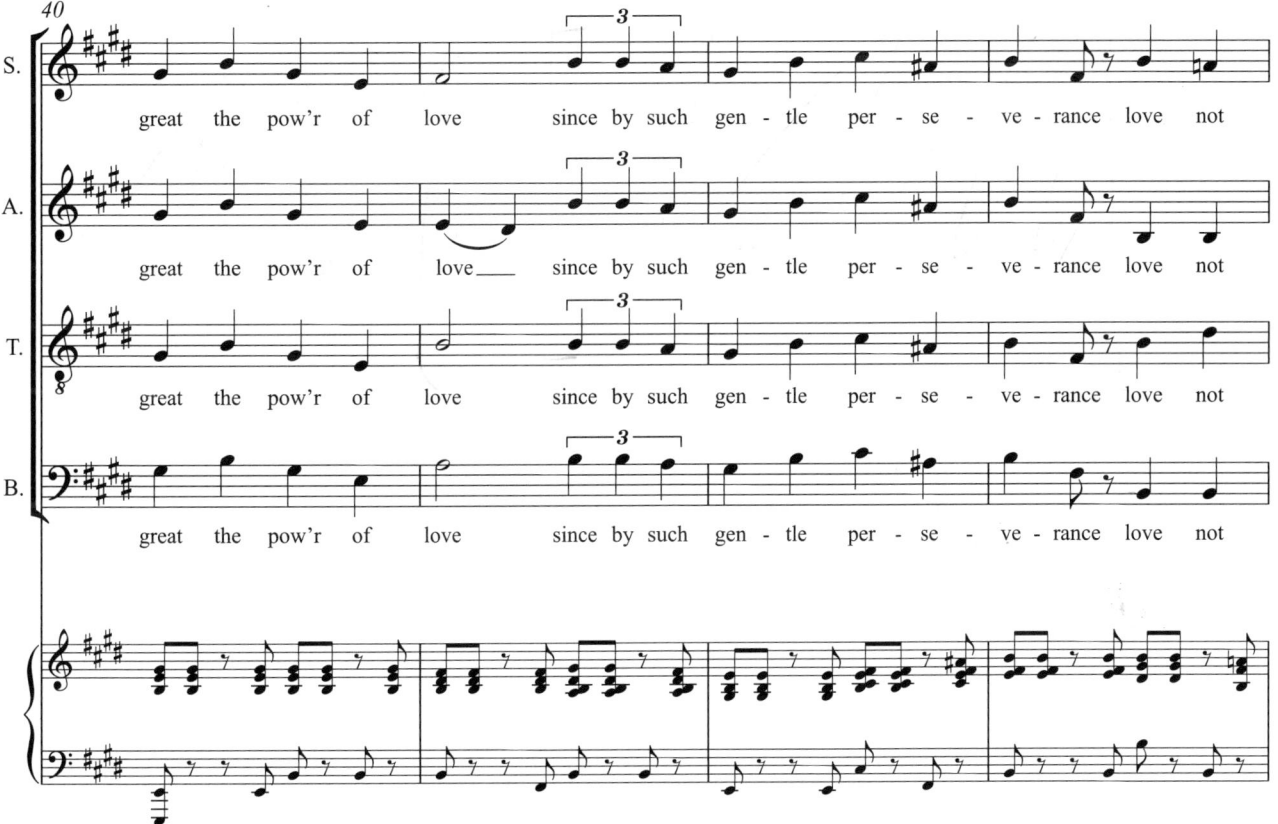

1. Romance of the Angels

52
S.
A.
T.
B.
f
3
Er - es ni - ño y has a - mor: qué fa - rás cuan - do
- dí - a: Er - es ni - ño__ y has a - mor:____ qué fa - rás cuan - do
Er - es ni - ño y has a - mor: qué fa - rás cuan - do
Er - es ni - ño__ y has a - mor: qué fa - rás cuan - do

56
S.
A.
T.
B.
3
ma - yor? You a child sur - round-ed by love; what great joy will your
ma - yor? You a child__ sur - round-ed by love;____ what great joy will your
ma - yor? You a child sur - round-ed by love; what great joy will your
ma - yor? You a child__ sur - round-ed by love; what great joy will your

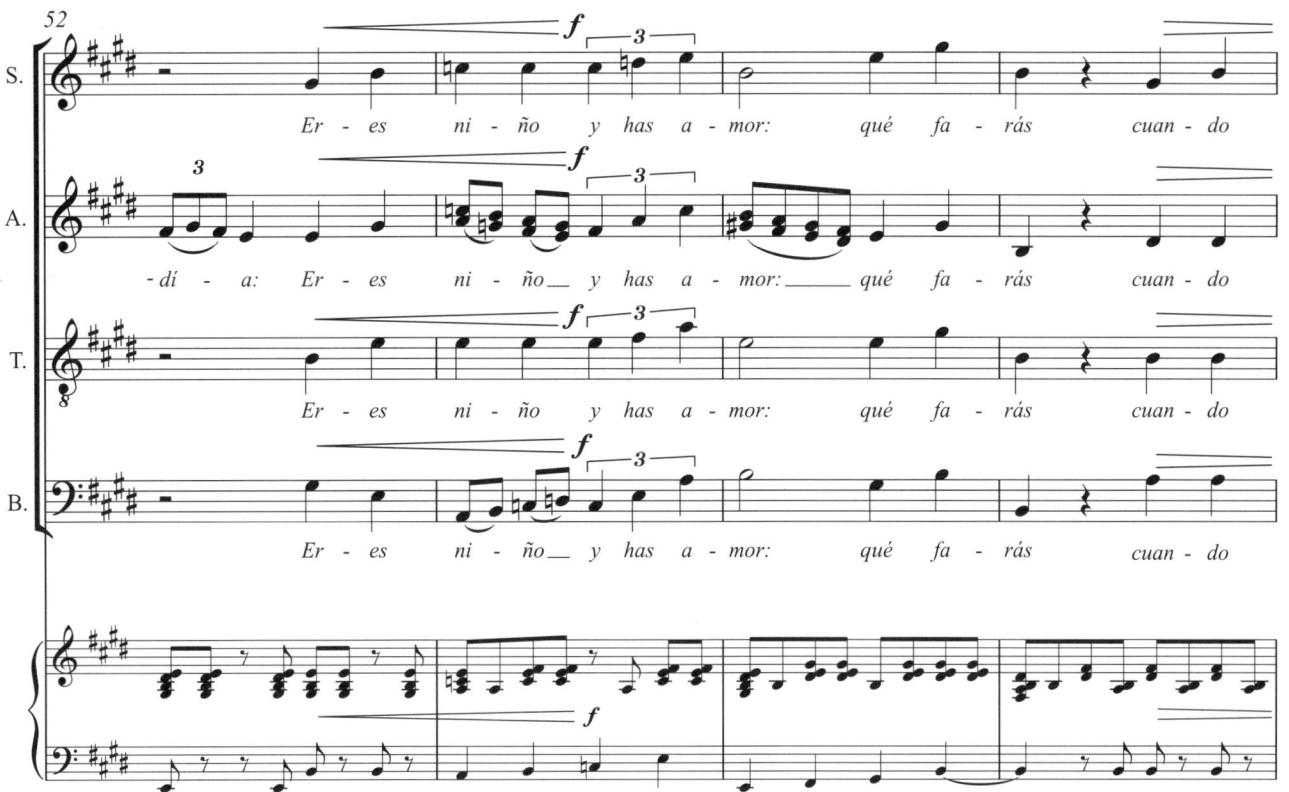

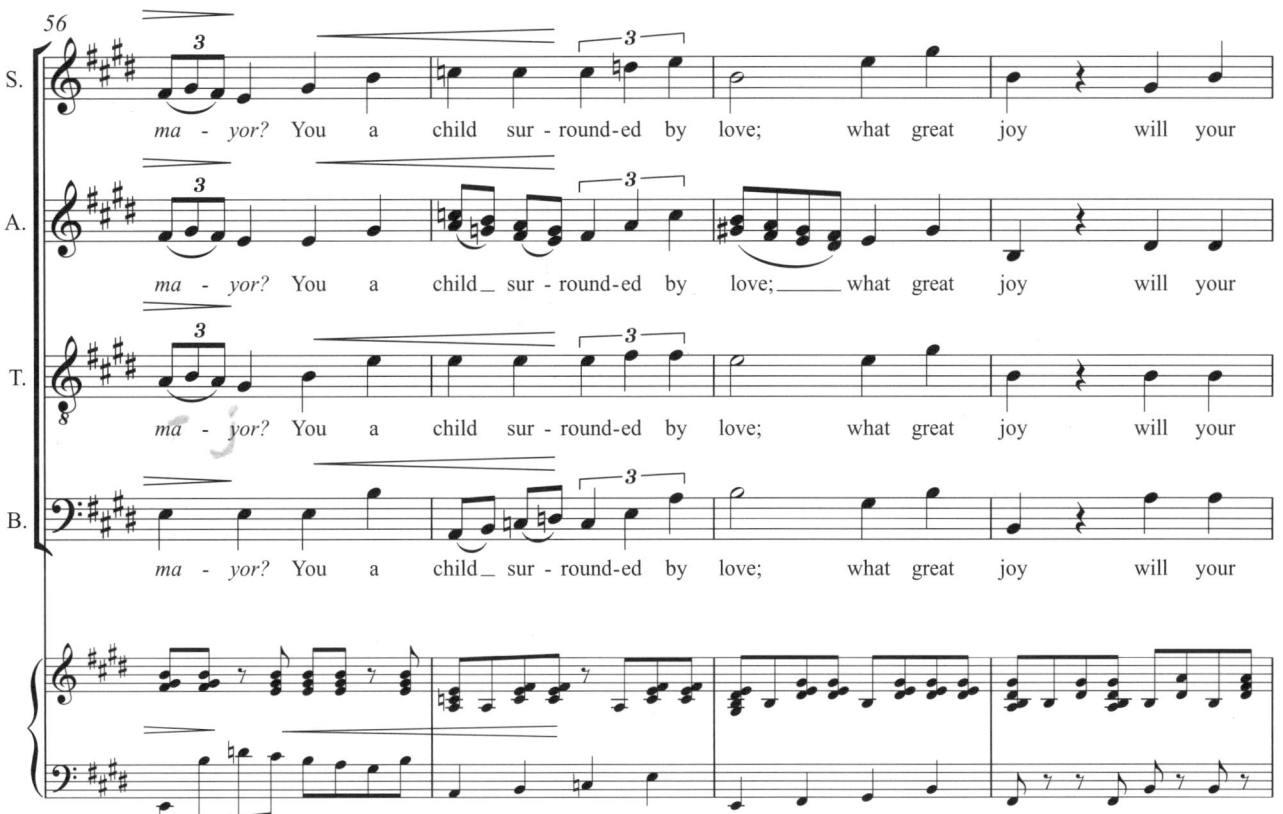

1. Romance of the Angels

10
1. Romance of the Angels

1. Romance of the Angels

1. Romance of the Angels

1. Romance of the Angels

13

14
1. Romance of the Angels

18   1. Romance of the Angels

1. Romance of the Angels

20

1. Romance of the Angels

2. Stella, quam viderant Magi

The Wise Men and the Star

Anon.

Howard Goodall

2. Stella, quam viderant Magi

2. Stella, quam viderant Magi

23

2. Stella, quam viderant Magi

48
S.
T.
mp
Stel - la quam vi - de-rant Ma - gi ab
Stel - la quam vi - de-rant Ma - gi ab

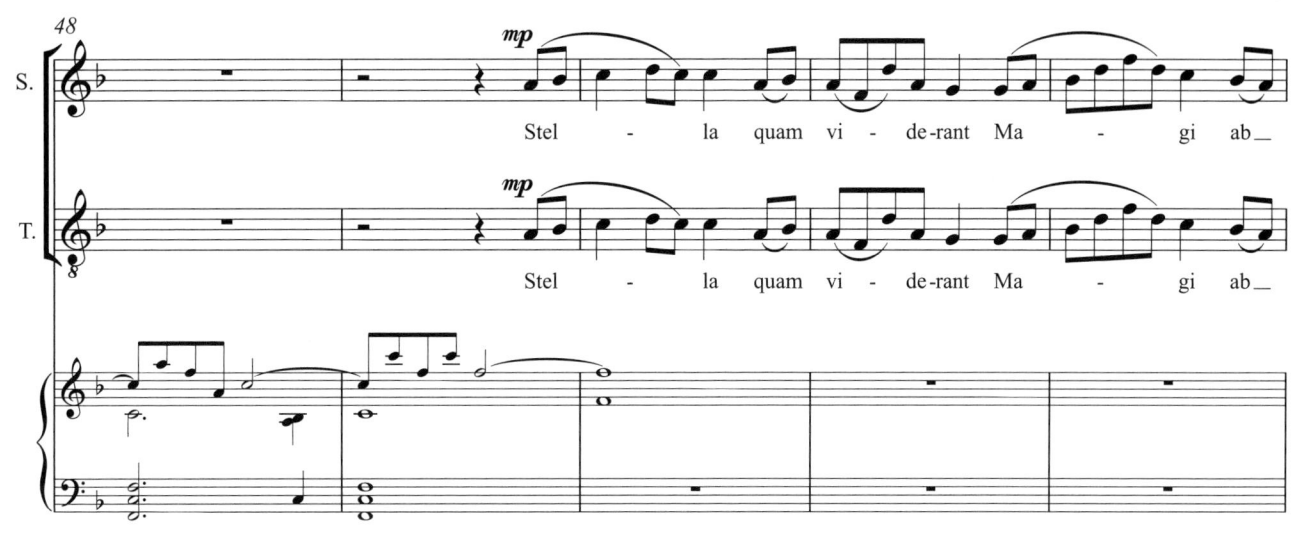

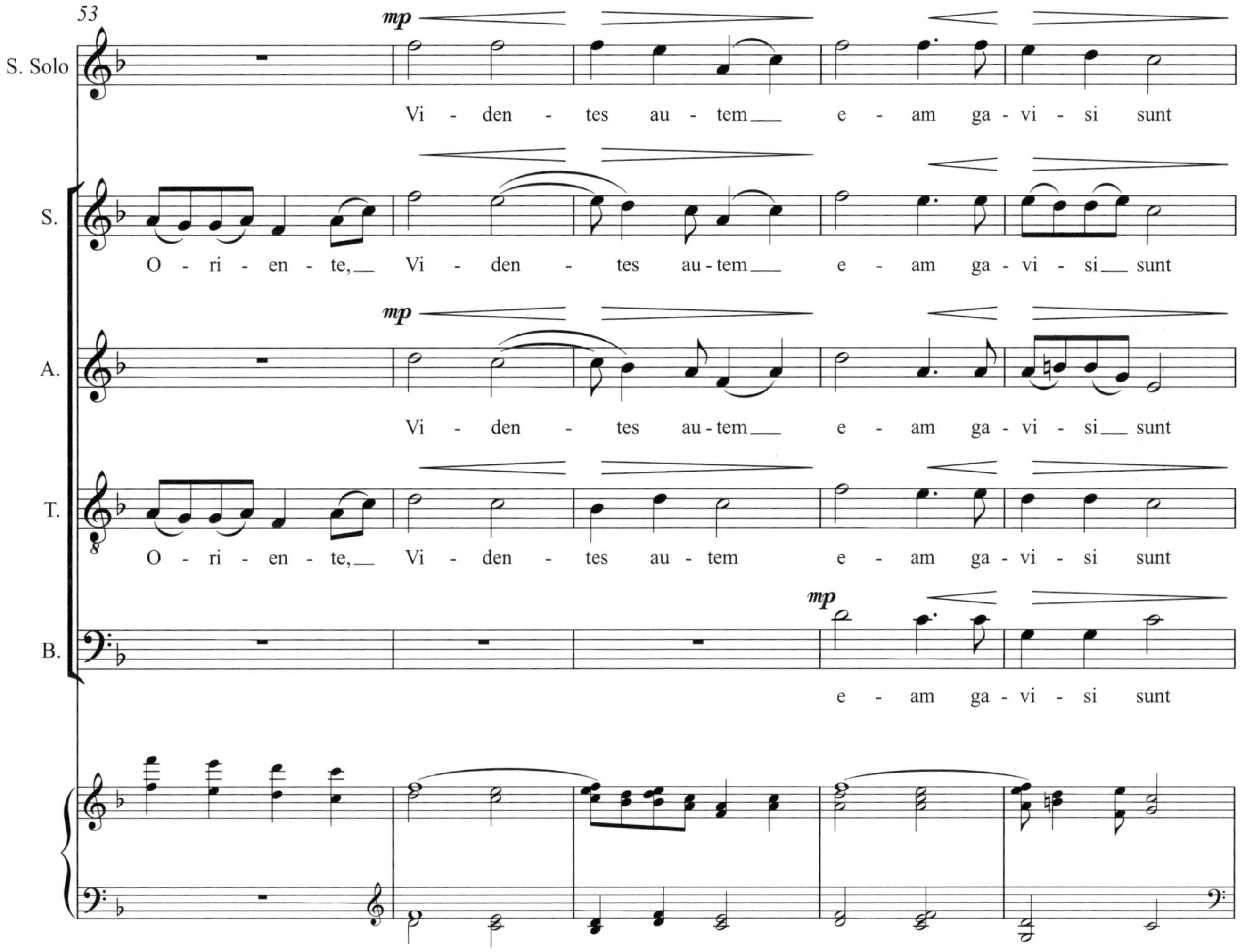
53
S. Solo
S.
A.
T.
B.
mp
Vi - den - tes au - tem e - am ga - vi - si sunt
O - ri - en - te, Vi - den - tes au - tem e - am ga - vi - si sunt
Vi - den - tes au - tem e - am ga - vi - si sunt
O - ri - en - te, Vi - den - tes au - tem e - am ga - vi - si sunt
e - am ga - vi - si sunt

26 2. Stella, quam viderant Magi

2. Stella, quam viderant Magi

28

3. It Came Upon the Midnight Clear

Edmund H Sears (1810-1876)
W Evans Jones (1854-1938)

Howard Goodall

© 2016 by Faber Music Ltd.
This edition © 2021 by Faber Music Ltd.

3. It Came Upon the Midnight Clear

3. It Came Upon the Midnight Clear

3. It Came Upon the Midnight Clear

3. It Came Upon the Midnight Clear

strain have rolled two thou-sand years of wrong; And

man, at war with man, hears not The love-song which they bring; O

3. It Came Upon the Midnight Clear

3. It Came Upon the Midnight Clear

35

rest be-side the wea-ry road, And hear the an-gels sing! O

rest be-side the wea-ry road, And hear the an-gels sing! O

rest be-side the wea-ry road, And hear the an-gels sing! O

rest be-side the wea-ry road, And hear the an-gels sing!

Ah

hush the noise, ye men of strife And hear the an-gels sing.

hush the noise, ye men of strife And hear the an-gels sing.

And hear the an-gels sing. O

And hear the an-gels sing. O

Ah

3. It Came Upon the Midnight Clear

4. Lullaby of Winter

Words and music by
Howard Goodall

4. Lullaby of winter

S. Solo: fault-line where the cen-tu-ries col-lide The Ro-mans loathed them,___ those rest-less tribes,___ who on-ly had one God and He was on their side.

S.: Mm___

A.: Mm___

S. Solo: What do they mean, these ref-'ren-ces to pro-phets? They seem to

4. Lullaby of winter

re-in-force the claim that it's a fic-tion. Two wand-'ring Jews they were___ with no place to rest. A stink-ing cave would have to do, and stuff their pride. No doubt they

Ah___

Ah___

Ah___

4. Lullaby of winter

loved him, the ti-ny bairn, (the sleep-ing rough and be-ing des-ti-tute a-side). What does it mean, that i-con of the

4. Lullaby of winter

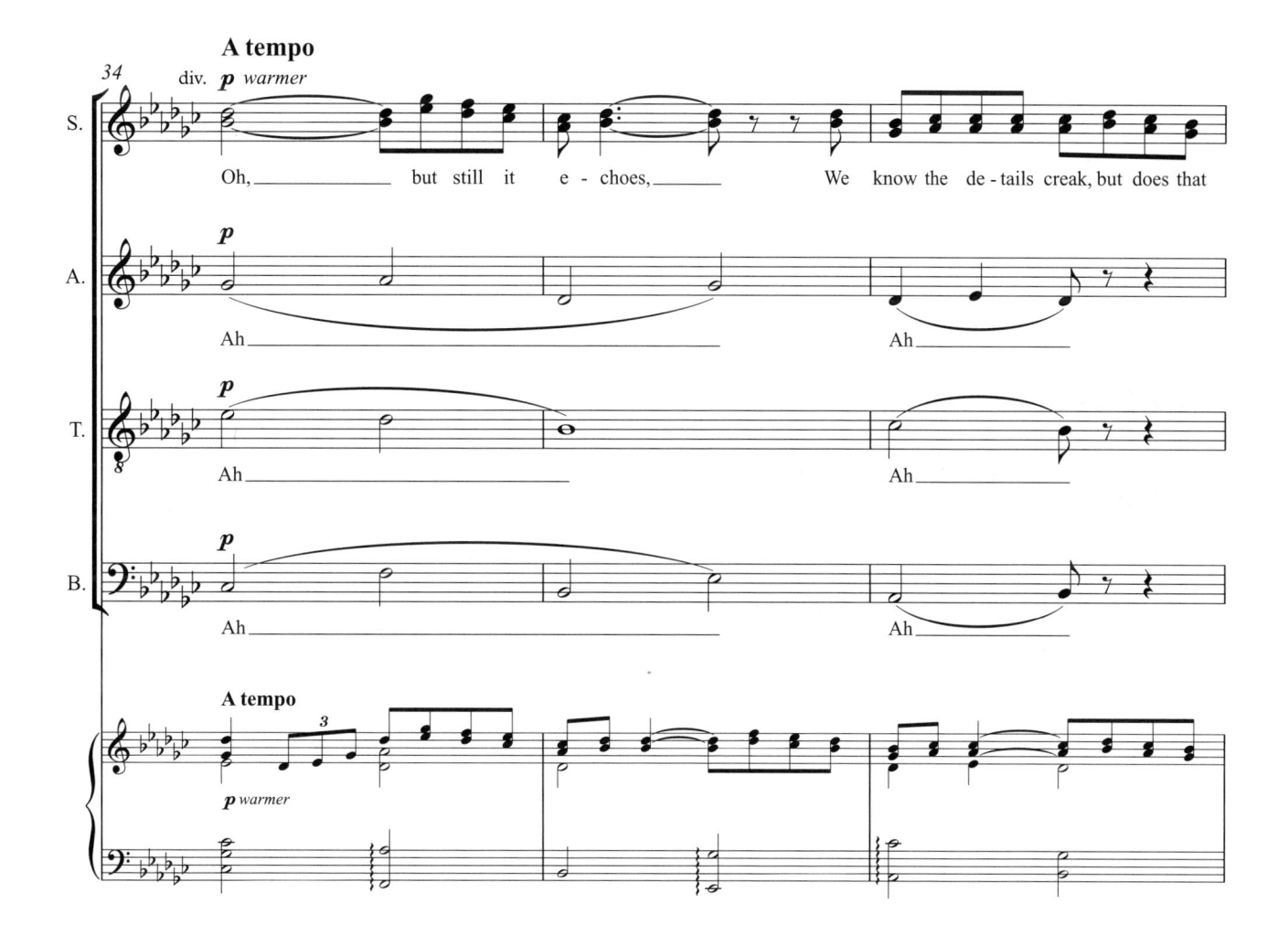

4. Lullaby of winter

4. Lullaby of winter

4. Lullaby of winter

4. Lullaby of winter

45

4. Lullaby of winter

S. Solo: -mind-ed of some truths that do not wane. That for each home-less girl like her there are two

S. Solo: end-ings: one where we hold her hand, a-no-ther where we don't.

S.: For ev-'ry
A.: For ev-'ry
T.: For ev-'ry
B.: For ev-'ry

4. Lullaby of winter

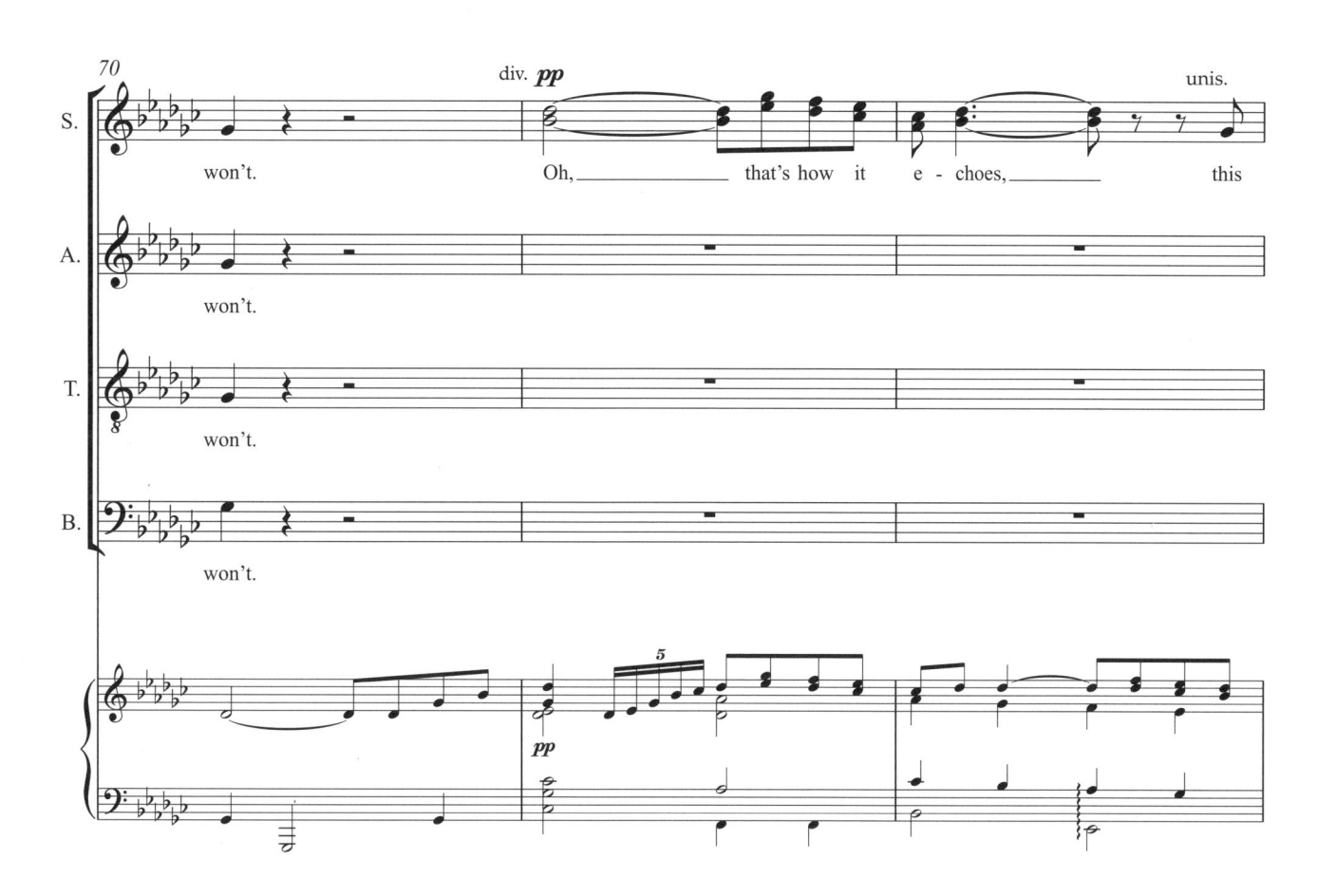

S: help-less kid like him there are two sto-ries: one where we heed the cry, a-no-ther where we
A: help-less kid like him there are two sto-ries: one where we heed the cry, a-no-ther where we
T: help-less kid like him there are two sto-ries: one where we heed the cry, a-no-ther where we
B: help-less kid like him there are two sto-ries: one where we heed the cry, a-no-ther where we

S: won't. Oh, that's how it e-choes, this
A: won't.
T: won't.
B: won't.

4. Lullaby of winter

4. Lullaby of winter

5. To See Another Sun

Giles Fletcher (1587–1623)
Howard Goodall

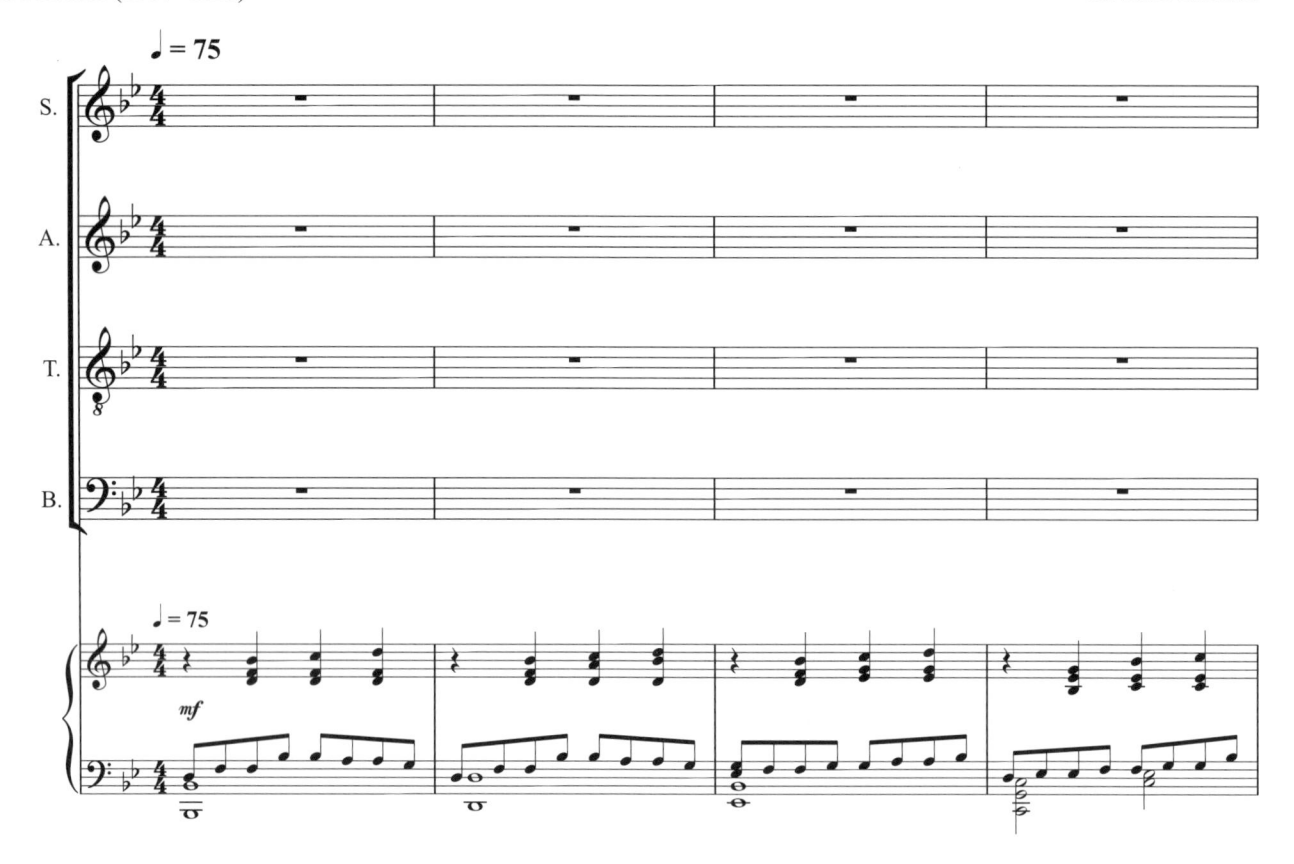

He is a path, if any be mis-led;

© 2003 by Faber Music Ltd.
This edition © 2021 by Faber Music Ltd.

5. To See Another Sun
51

5. To See Another Sun

he is free; If a-ny be but weak, how strong is he!

To dead men life he is, to sick men health; To blind men sight, and to the

5. To See Another Sun

S: nee-dy wealth; A plea-sure with-out loss, a trea-sure with-out
A: nee-dy wealth; A plea-sure with-out loss, a trea-sure with-out
T: nee-dy wealth; A plea-sure with-out loss, a trea-sure with-out
B: nee-dy wealth; A plea-sure with-out loss, a trea-sure with-out

S: stealth.
A: stealth.
T: stealth.
B: stealth.

5. To See Another Sun

S: Who can for-get, ne-ver to be for-got, The time when all the world in slum-ber
A: Who can for-get, ne-ver to be for-got, The time when all the world in slum-ber
T: Who can for-get, ne-ver to be for-got, The time when all the world in slum-ber
B: Who can for-get, ne-ver to be for-got, The time when all the world in slum-ber

S: lies. When like stars, the sing-ing an-gels shot To earth, and
A: lies. When like stars, the sing-ing an-gels shot To earth, and
T: lies. When like stars, the sing-ing an-gels shot To earth, and
B: lies. When like stars, the sing-ing an-gels shot To earth, and

5. To See Another Sun

5. To See Another Sun

rise. rise. rise. rise.

A child he was, and had not learnt to
That
A child he was, and had not learnt to
That

5. To See Another Sun

speak, His mother's arms him bore, he was so
with his word the world before did make; That
speak, His mother's arms him bore, he was so
with his word the world before did make; That

weak, See how small room my infant Lord doth
with one hand the vaults of heav'n could shake. Whom
weak, See how small room my infant Lord doth
with one hand the vaults of heav'n could shake. Whom

5. To See Another Sun

S: take, Who of his years, or of his age, hath told?
A: all the world is not e-nough to hold.
T: take, Who of his years, or of his age, hath told?
B: all the world is not e-nough to hold.

S: never a child so
A: never a child so
T: Never such age so young, never a child so
B: Never such age so young, never a child so

5. To See Another Sun

59

S.: old, ne - ver a child so old. He is a
A.: old, ne - ver a child so old. He is a
T.: old, ne - ver a child so old. He is a
B.: old, ne - ver a child so old. He is a

S.: path, if a - ny be mis - led;
A.: path, if a - ny be mis - led;
T.: path, if a - ny be mis - led;
B.: path, if a - ny be mis - led;

5. To See Another Sun

S.: He is a robe, if a-ny na-ked be;
A.: He is a robe, if a-ny na-ked be;
T.: He is a robe, if a-ny na-ked be;
B.: He is a robe, if a-ny na-ked be;

S.: Who can for-get, ne-ver to be for-
A.: Who can for-get, ne-ver to be for-
T.: Who can for-get, ne-ver to be for-
B.: Who can for-get, ne-ver to be for-

5. To See Another Sun

5. To See Another Sun

S: see a - no - ther Sun at mid - night rise,_____
A: see a - no - ther Sun at mid - night rise,_____
T: see a - no - ther Sun at mid - night rise,_____
B: see a - no - ther Sun at mid - night rise,_____

S: _____ a - no - ther Sun at mid - night rise, When, like
A: _____ a - no - ther Sun at mid - night rise, When, like
T: _____ a - no - ther Sun at mid - night rise, When, like
B: _____ a - no - ther Sun at mid - night rise, When, like

5. To See Another Sun

stars, the sing-ing an-gels shot To earth, and heav'n a-wak-éd all his eyes, To see a-no-ther Sun at mid-night rise.

6. Romance of the Epiphany

Romance día de la Epifanía, descubierto el Santísimo Sacramento

José de Valdivielso (1565-1638)
Trans. Howard Goodall

Howard Goodall

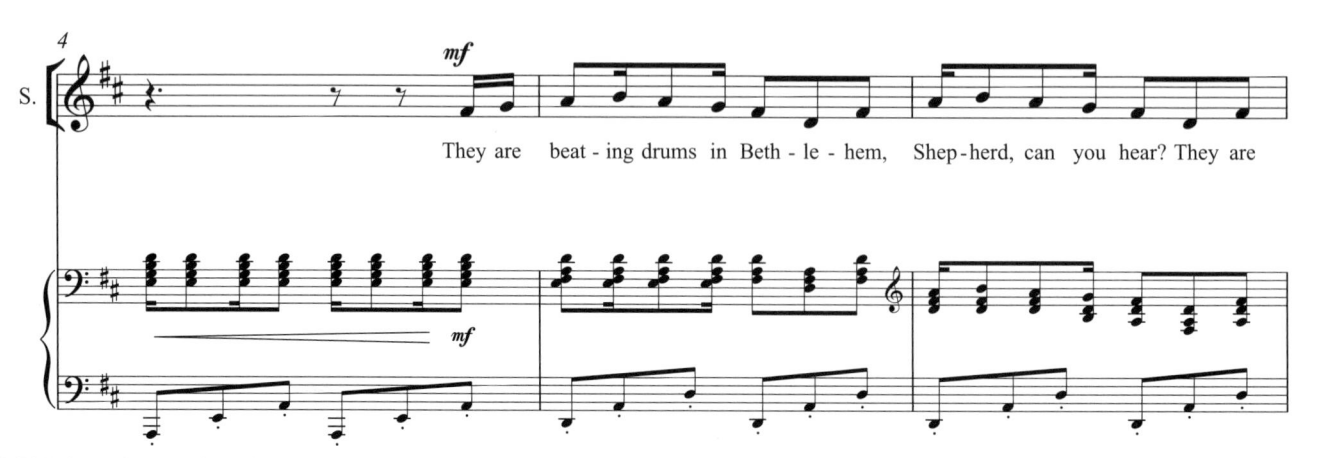

They are beat-ing drums in Beth-le-hem, Shep-herd, can you hear? They are

© 2012 by Faber Music Ltd.
This edition © 2021 by Faber Music Ltd.

6. Romance of the Epiphany

65

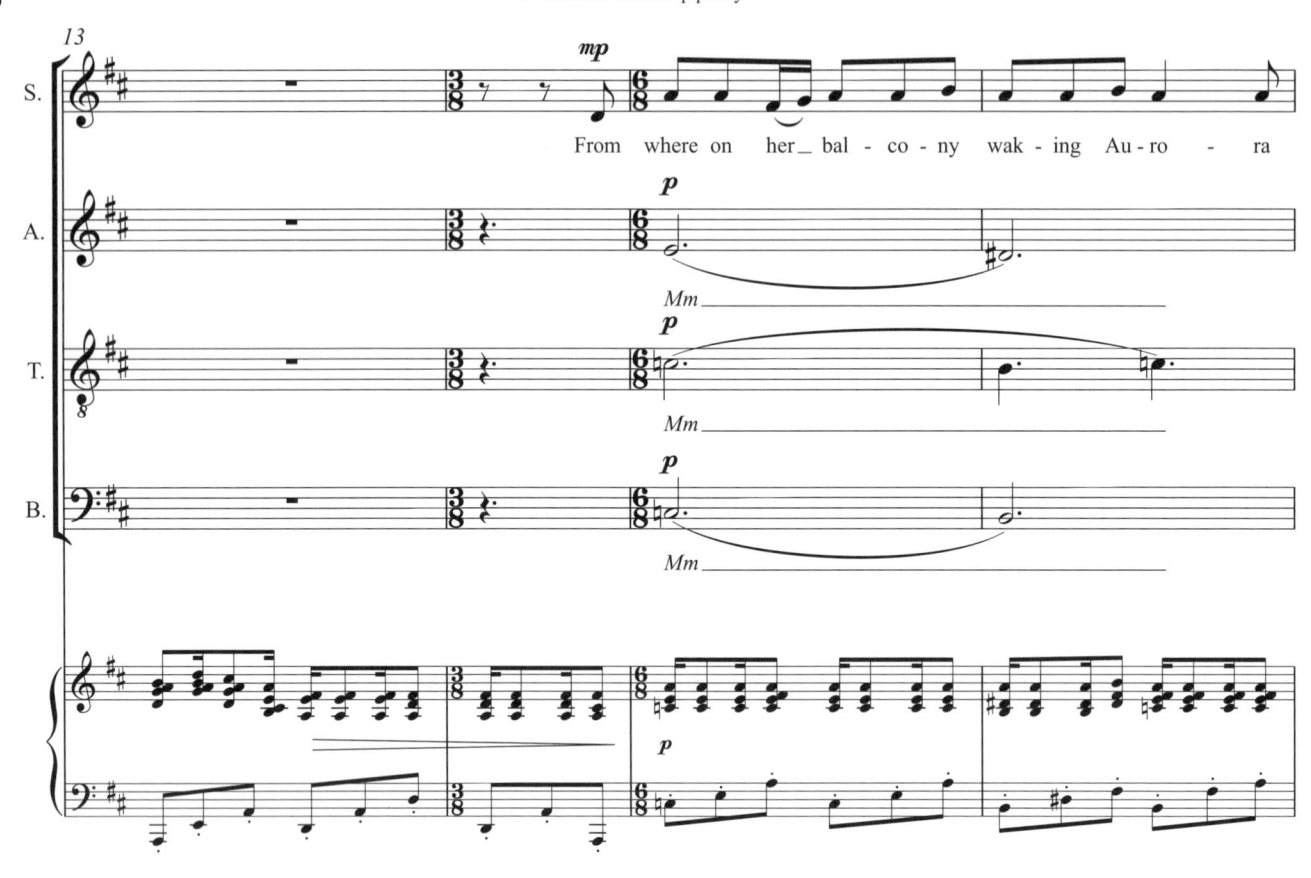

6. Romance of the Epiphany

S.: From where on her bal-co-ny wak-ing Au-ro-ra smiles as she brings out the rays of the sun,

A.: Mm___ mm___

T.: Mm___ mm___ comes Bal-tha-sar, Gas-par, Mel-chi-or too, they are

B.: Mm___ comes Bal-tha-sar, Gas-par, Mel-chi-or too, they are

6. Romance of the Epiphany

6. Romance of the Epiphany

6. Romance of the Epiphany

S: Shep-herd, can you hear? They are play-ing lit-tle trum-pets, their sound re-joi-ces me! A - ta -
A: A - ta -
T: Shep-herd, can you hear? They are play-ing lit-tle trum-pets, their sound re-joi-ces me! A - ta -
B: A - ta -

S/A/T/B: -ba - les to-can en Be - lén, Pas - tor, Trom-pe - ti-cas su - e-nan a - lé -

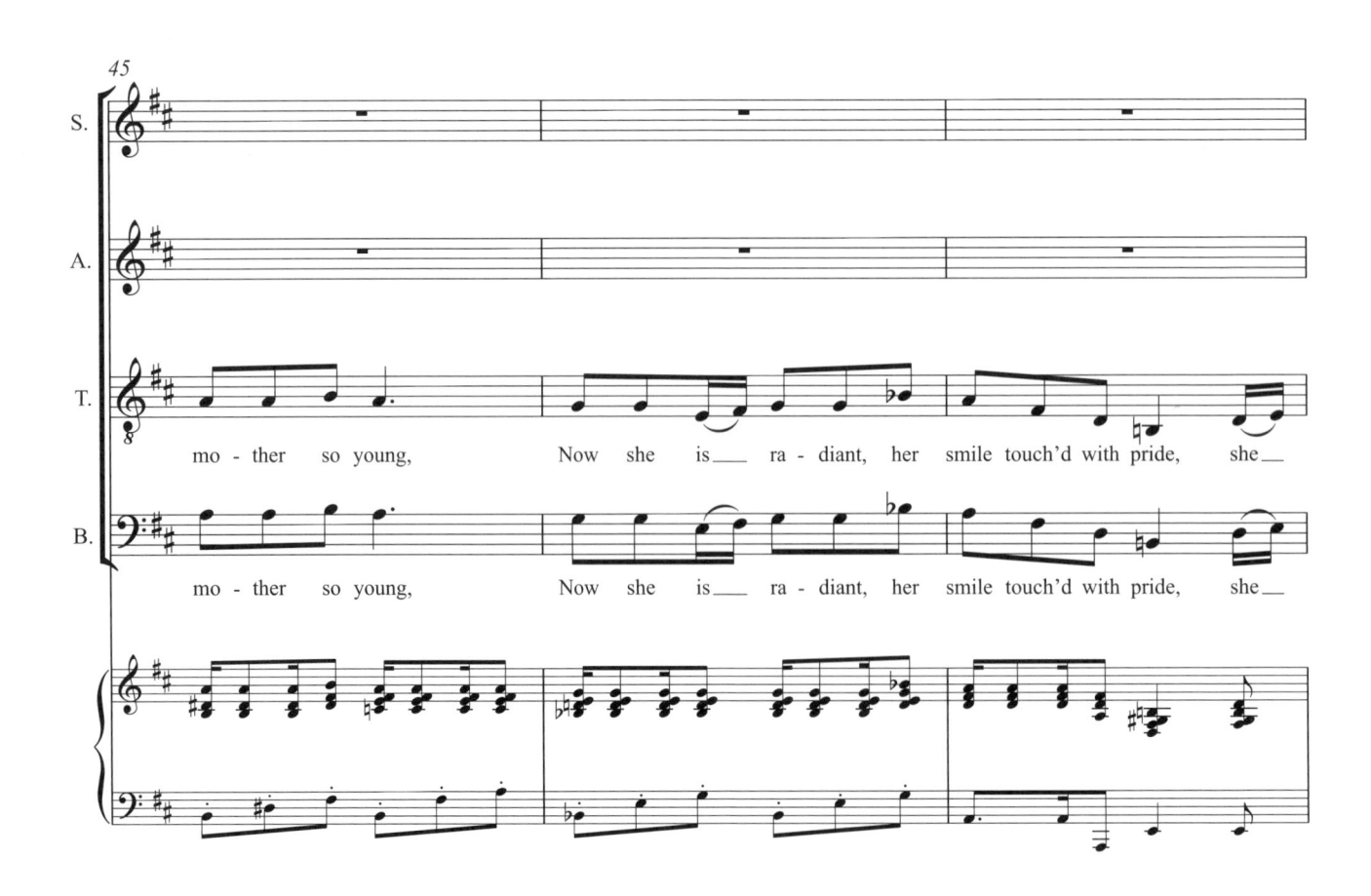

6. Romance of the Epiphany

S. -gra-me el— son!

A. -gra-me el— son!

T. -gra-me el— son! King So-lo-mon told of a

B. -gra-me el— son! King So-lo-mon told of a

T. mo-ther so young, Now she is— ra-diant, her smile touch'd with pride, she—

B. mo-ther so young, Now she is— ra-diant, her smile touch'd with pride, she—

6. Romance of the Epiphany

T: glows with a ha - lo of stars round a - bout, her mantle of shin - ing gems
B: glows with a ha - lo of stars round a - bout, her mantle of shin - ing gems

S: Y un man - to de lust - ro con puntas de sol.
A: Y un man - to de lust - ro con puntas de sol. For her
T: ring'd by the sun, Y un man - to de lust - ro con puntas de sol. For her
B: ring'd by the sun, Y un man - to de lust - ro con puntas de sol.

6. Romance of the Epiphany

slip-pers, em-broi-der'd with sap-phire and silk, the moon gave her sil-ver from

slip-pers, em-broi-der'd with sap-phire and silk, the moon gave her sil-ver from

the moon gave her sil-ver from

mo-

hea-ven it-self, her hair is em-bla-zon'd with ru-by and jade, mo-

hea-ven it-self, her hair is em-bla-zon'd with ru-by and jade, mo-

hea-ven it-self, her hair is em-bla-zon'd with ru-by and jade, mo-

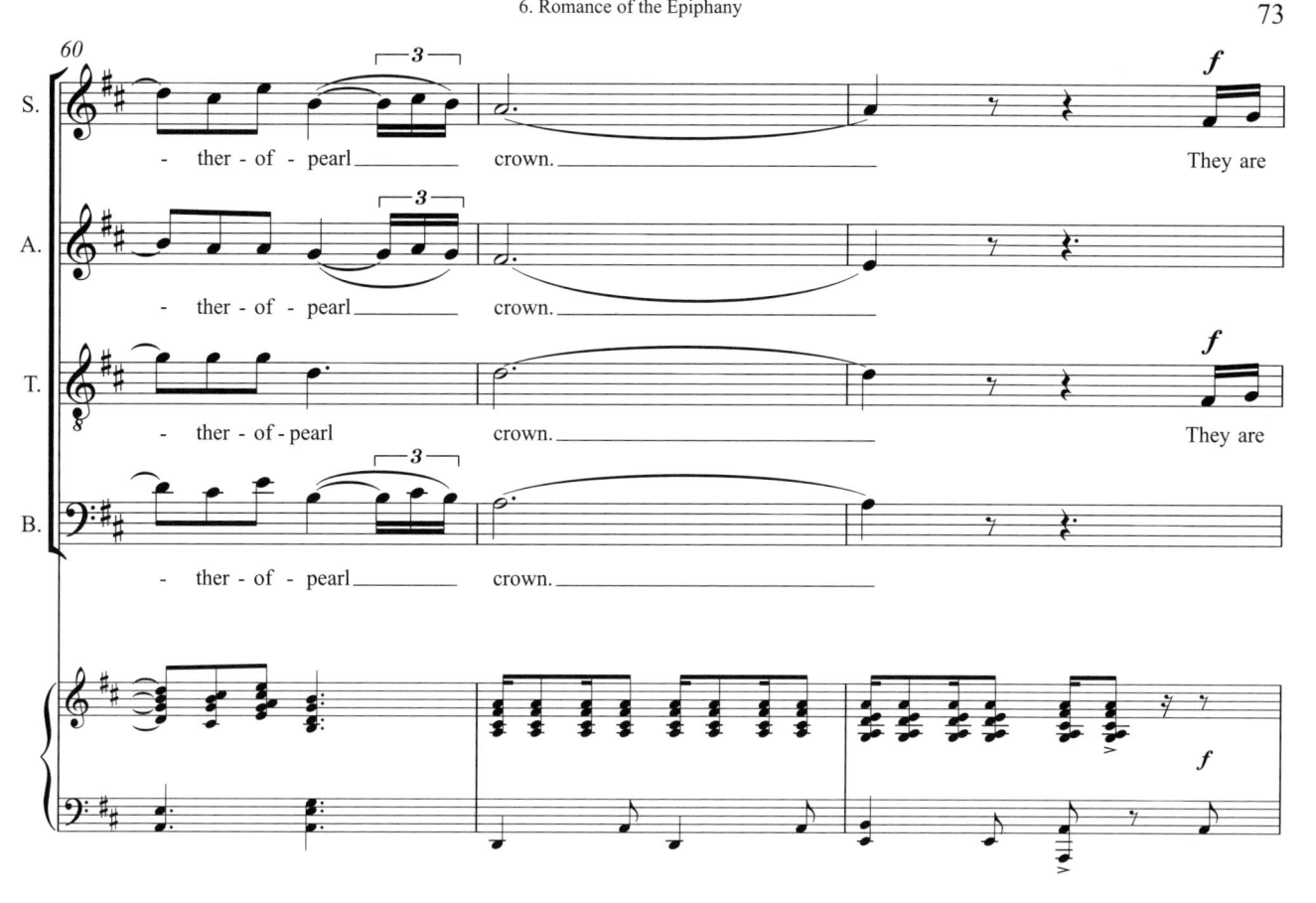

6. Romance of the Epiphany

-ther-of-pearl crown. They are

-ther-of-pearl crown.

-ther-of-pearl crown. They are

-ther-of-pearl crown.

beat-ing drums in Beth-le-hem, Shep-herd, can you hear? They are play-ing lit-tle trum-pets, their

beat-ing drums in Beth-le-hem, Shep-herd, can you hear? They are play-ing lit-tle trum-pets, their

6. Romance of the Epiphany

S: sound re-joi-ces me! A-ta-ba-les to-can en Be-lén, Pas-tor, Trom-pe-
A: A-ta-ba-les to-can en Be-lén, Pas-tor, Trom-pe-
T: sound re-joi-ces me! A-ta-ba-les to-can en Be-lén, Pas-tor, Trom-pe-
B: A-ta-ba-les to-can en Be-lén, Pas-tor, Trom-pe-

S: -ti-cas su-e-nan a-lé-gra-me el son!
A: -ti-cas su-e-nan a-lé-gra-me el son!
T: -ti-cas su-e-nan a-lé-gra-me el son!
B: -ti-cas su-e-nan a-lé-gra-me el son!

6. Romance of the Epiphany

75

From the earth and from the hea-vens, she brought out the best, a stone Ag-nus De-i hung round her white neck, the pret-ty child cried out at the

Ag-nus De-i the pret-ty child cried out at the

Ag-nus De-i

Ag-nus De-i

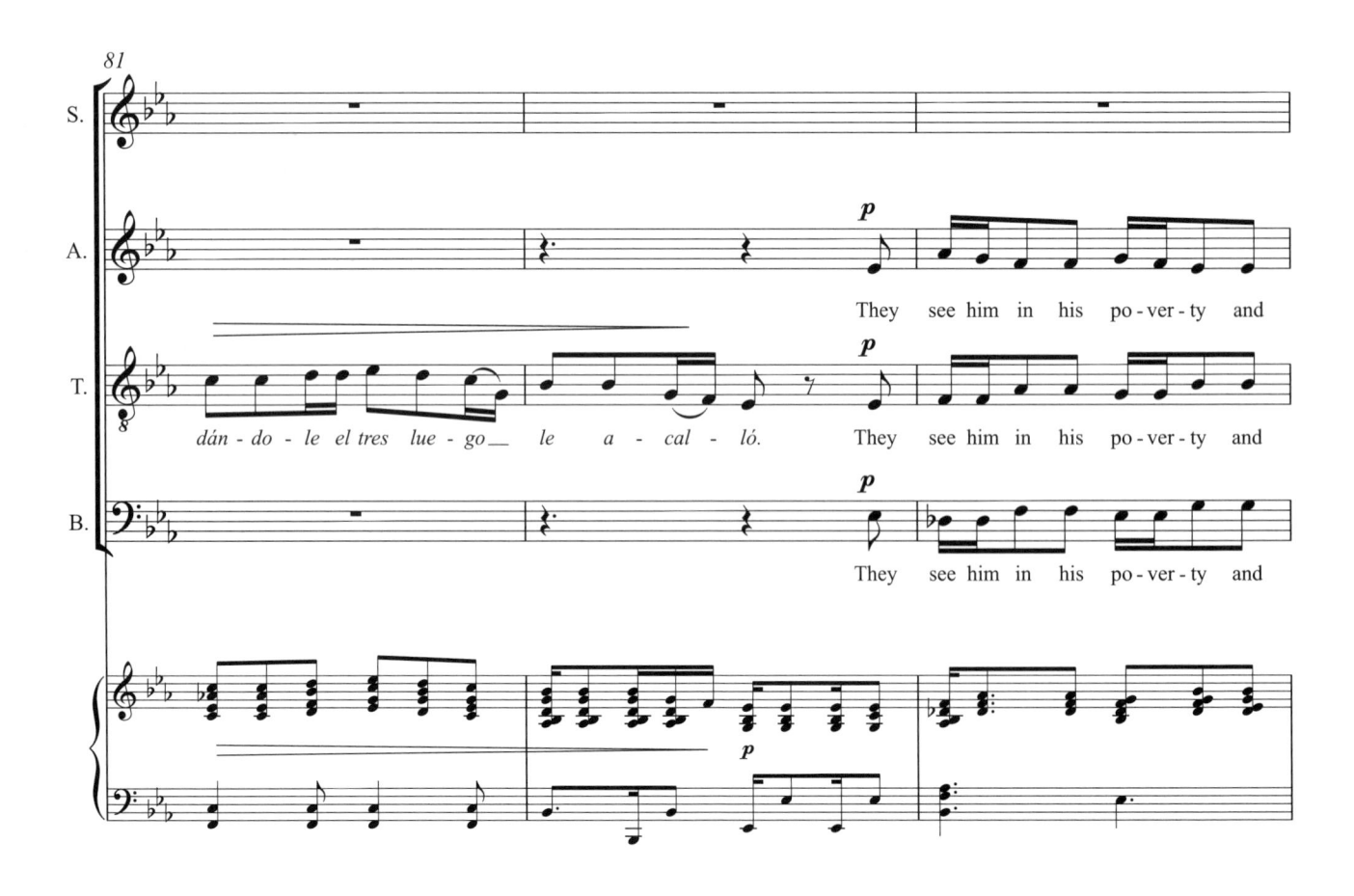

6. Romance of the Epiphany

S: harsh win-ter frost but she soon made him sound-less with gifts from the Kings.

A: harsh win-ter frost but she soon made him sound-less with gifts from the Kings.

T: gifts from the Kings, Mas-

B: but she soon made him sound-less with gifts from the Kings.

A: They see him in his po-ver-ty and

T: dán-do-le el tres lue-go le a-cal-ló. They see him in his po-ver-ty and

B: They see him in his po-ver-ty and

6. Romance of the Epiphany

6. Romance of the Epiphany

S: souls. — They are beat-ing drums in Beth-le-hem,
A: souls. — They are beat-ing drums in Beth-le-hem,
T: souls. — They are beat-ing drums in Beth-le-hem,
B: souls. — They are beat-ing drums in Beth-le-hem,

S: Shep-herd, can you hear? They are play-ing lit-tle trum-pets, their sound re-joi-ces me! A - ta -
A: Shep-herd, can you hear? They are play-ing lit-tle trum-pets, their sound re-joi-ces me! A - ta -
T: Shep-herd, can you hear? They are play-ing lit-tle trum-pets, their sound re-joi-ces me! A - ta -
B: Shep-herd, can you hear? They are play-ing lit-tle trum-pets, their sound re-joi-ces me! A - ta -

6. Romance of the Epiphany

-ba - les to-can en Be - lén, Pas - tor, Trom-pe - ti - cas su - e - nan a - le - gra - me el son! They are beat - ing drums in Beth - le - hem, Shep-herd, can you hear? They are

6. Romance of the Epiphany

playing little trumpets, their sound rejoices me! A-ta-ba-les to-can en Be-lén, Pas-tor, Trom-pe-ti-cas su-e-nan a-lé-gra-me el son!

7. I am Christmas Day

Words and music by
Howard Goodall

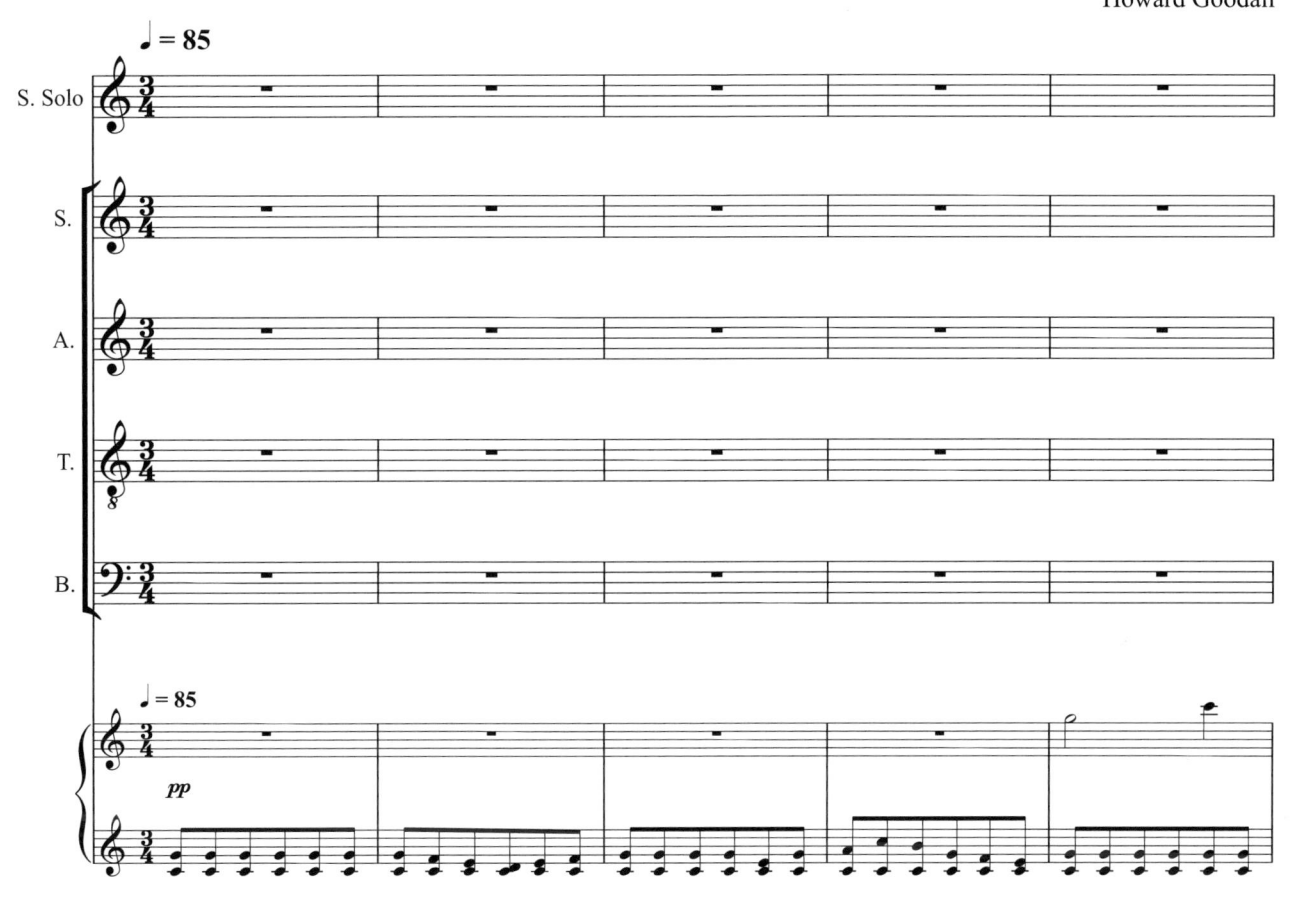

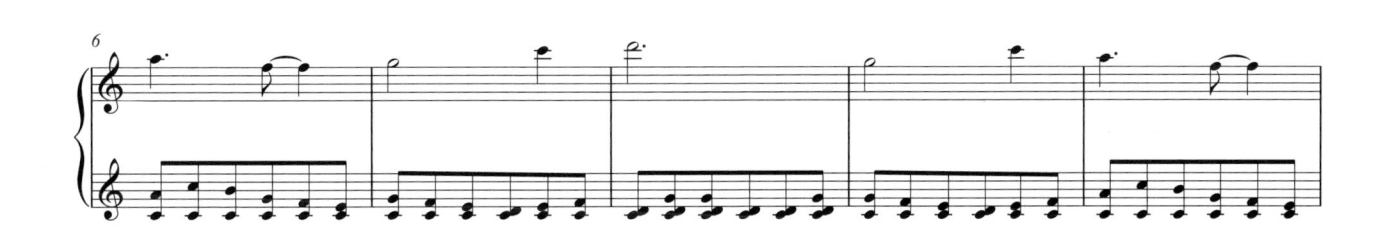

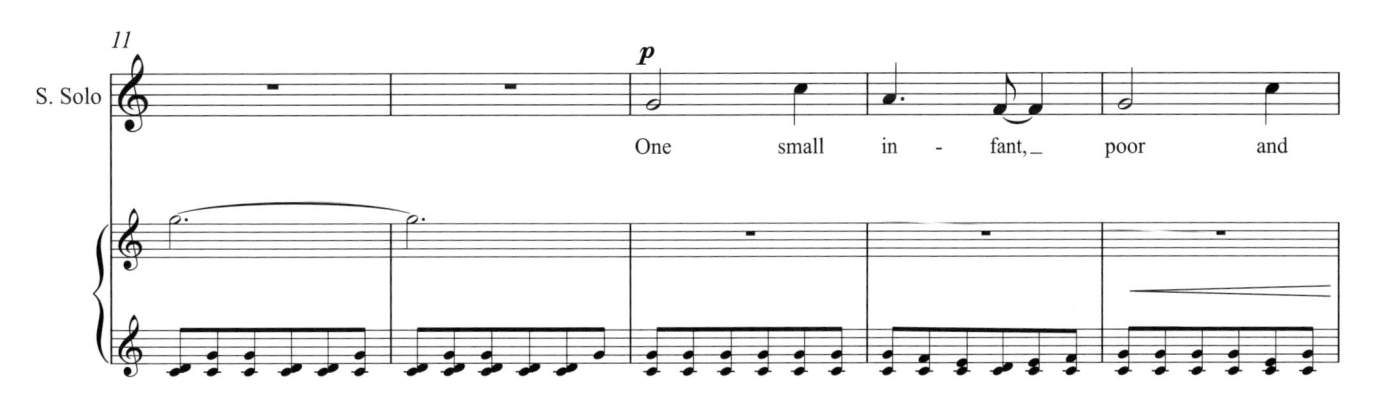

One small in-fant, poor and

7. I am Christmas Day

frail Two thou-sand years a - go, could be a mil-lion miles a-way One rough sta - ble, mea - gre shel-ter from the night. What's so spe-cial, what's the sto - ry here? Cent-'ries pass, yet still it seems to say:

poco rall.

7. I am Christmas Day

Ev-'ry child born, ev-'ry new dawn's a-no-ther Christ-mas Day.

Some-one's Christ-mas Day.

Some-where hope springs, one more heart sings, it's some-one's Christ-mas Day.

7. I am Christmas Day

7. I am Christmas Day

7. I am Christmas Day

S. All these de-tails pro-ba-bly have been built up,

A. All these de-tails pro-ba-bly have been built up,

T. All these de-tails pro-ba-bly have been built up,

B. All these de-tails pro-ba-bly have been built up,

poco rall.

S. None-the-less there is a mes-sage here: Born in hard-ship, one child changed the world.

A. None-the-less there is a mes-sage here: Born in hard-ship, one child changed the world.

T. None-the-less there is a mes-sage here: Born in hard-ship, one child changed the world.

B. None-the-less there is a mes-sage here: Born in hard-ship, one child changed the world.

poco rall.

7. I am Christmas Day

A tempo

S: Ev-'ry child born, ev-'ry new dawn's a-no-ther Christ-mas Day.

A: Ev-'ry child born, ev-'ry new dawn's a-no-ther Christ-mas Day.

T: Ev-'ry child born, ev-'ry new dawn's a-no-ther Christ-mas Day.

B: Ev-'ry child born, ev-'ry new dawn's a-no-ther Christ-mas Day.

S: Some-where hope springs, one more heart sings, it's some-one's Christ-mas Day.

A: Some-where hope springs, one more heart sings, it's some-one's Christ-mas Day.

T: Some-where hope springs, one more heart sings, it's some-one's Christ-mas Day.

B: Some-where hope springs, one more heart sings, it's some-one's Christ-mas Day.

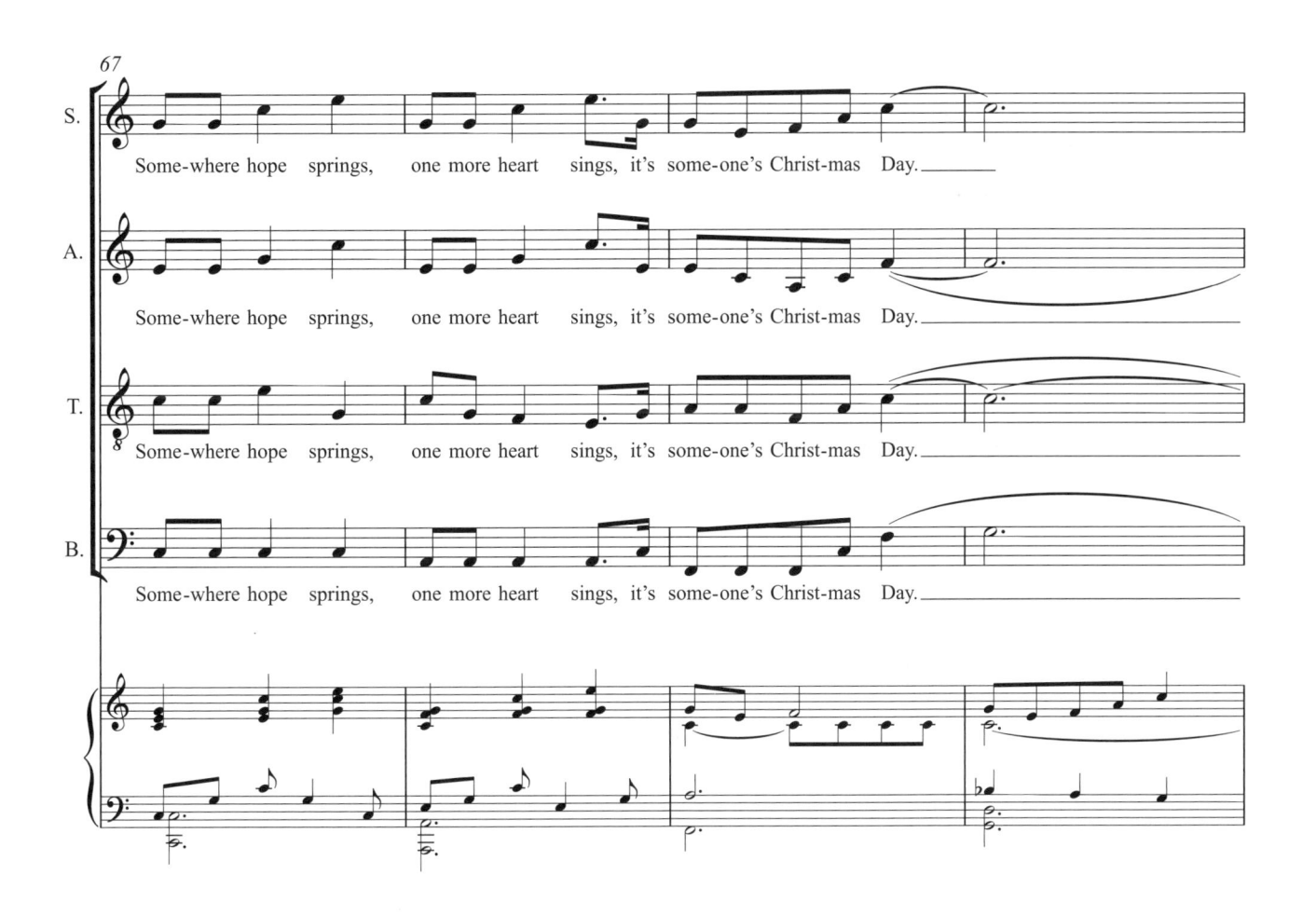

7. I am Christmas Day

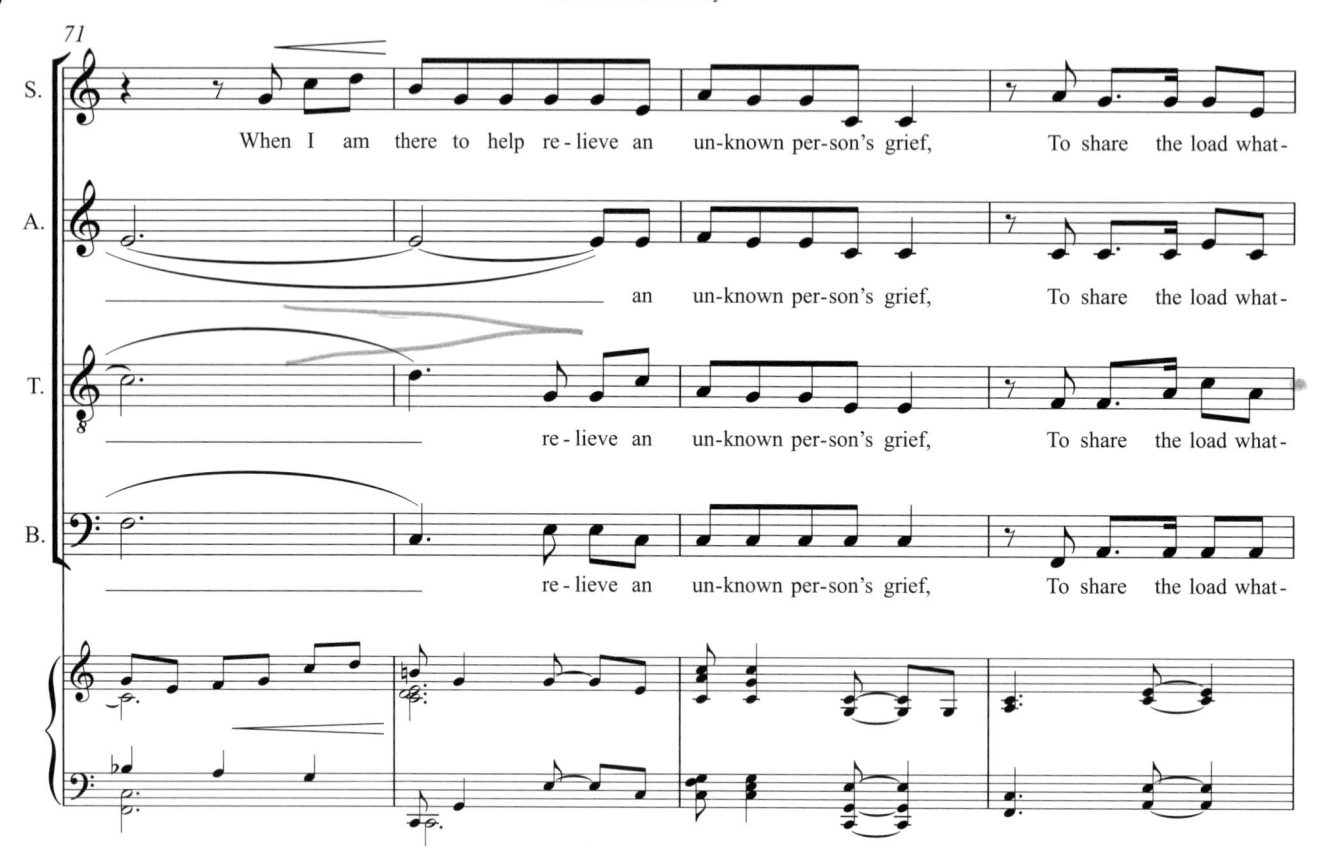

7. I am Christmas Day

7. I am Christmas Day

poco rall

S, A, T, B: sun go down on you, To feel your pain and ask what I can do...

poco rall

S. Solo: I am Christ - mas Day   I am Christ - mas,   I am Christ - mas,
S: I am Christ - mas Day   I am Christ - mas,   I am Christ - mas,
A: I am Christ - mas Day.   I am Christ - mas,   I am Christ - mas,
T: I am Christ - mas Day.   I am Christ - mas,   I am Christ - mas,
B: I am Christ - mas Day.   I am Christ - mas,   I am Christ - mas,

7. I am Christmas Day